THE D

THE DOCK STREET STORY

by

DENYS PARSONS

GOLDLEAF PUBLISHING
Port Talbot

ISBN 0 907117 71 6

Printed in Great Britain by
John Penri Press, Swansea

Foreword

I was born one of eight children. My parents, Ernie and Eva Parsons, had seven boys and one girl, my sister who was born just before my father went to join the Army. I was born in 1934, and this is the true story of the years when I lived in Dock Street, from 1934 to 1955.

I would like to thank all those people who helped me and supplied me with photographs of Dock Street. The poems included herein were written in memory of those who are not with us today.

Lastly, I would like to dedicate this book to Jimmy, Ceinwen, Raymond and Richard.

Chapter One

Although I was very young when the Second World War broke out, I can remember how we lived in Dock Street before 1939.

Dock Street was built around 1898, for the dock and railway workers, and consisted of twenty-five houses; it stood on the south-eastern side of Port Talbot docks, with its back against a railway embankment and its front facing the Betsy Pool and Morfa Beach. The area in front of the houses was a large warren, with green fields and streams running into the Betsy Pool, and there were otters, ducks, wild geese and rabbits in plenty, so that we became experts in the habits of these animals and any other wild-life round about.

The Betsy Pool was like a lagoon with the tide running in and out of it; when the tide was out, there was clear water and we used to walk about in this, chasing flatfish with a pointed stick (and often catching them!). When the tide was in, though, it was a very dangerous place to swim in, and many people lost their lives there, being carried out on the strong current and drowned. From the Betsy Pool to the stone pier we had a lovely pebble beach which we called 'Dock Street Beach'. There were large sandy tumps which were the home of dewberries and rabbits (which often landed on our Sunday dinner plates) and was a fine place for courting couples.

Mrs. Tooze, an old lady who lived at Number 2, Dock Street, kept a small shop there, which sold pop, potatoes and sweets, and later on Evan Jenkins opened another one, on his allotment (not in his house); he had to be on his toes when we boys came in. Before my time Mrs. McCann had a small farm in front of the street, and later Tom Keogh farmed there. He had a large family, all girls except for one boy, and Agnes, one of his daughters, had the job of taking the cattle out early in the morning. In the evening she would lead them home, and we all noticed how hard she worked.

Dock Street was a happy place then. Every door would be left open and people would walk in and out of the houses, borrowing cups of sugar and chatting to each other over a cup of tea while they sat on their doorsteps. On Saturday nights our fathers would go over to the Dock Hotel and come home merry; in the summertime someone would bring out a wireless (the old-fashioned dry battery kind) and there would be dancing and singing in the street. We kids be hanging out of our bedroom windows and would see them all singing their heads off.

It is good to think back to those wonderful times when people trusted each other and every door was open to everyone. People helped each other then, through all the hard times, and I am glad that I was brought up in that generation of happiness.

Sport was very important to us then. The Dock Stars football team was formed in about 1905; they had a ground at the top of the street and hundreds would come to watch them there. I believe they used to change in the houses in the street. The quality of football was very high in those days, and in the Twenties the Stars were very rarely beaten – indeed, for a couple of years they had an unbeaten record. (I was only a small boy then, but I still remember the excitement when they were playing).

There were some remarkable characters in those days – for instance, Jim Herbert, who can be seen in the middle of the photograph of the very first Dock Stars team. And then there was John Charles who played for the Stars for many years; he was living in Newbridge Road until his death last year when he was in his nineties, and was then the oldest living former resident of Dock Street. The most outstanding player ever to play for the Dock Stars was Tommy Bamford, and though I was too young to remember him playing, he was a living legend to us boys. We heard stories of how he broke a cross bar when taking a penalty and how he could score from anywhere, with either foot. Soon the scouts were down looking at him and eventually he went to Manchester United and was capped for Wales; towards the end of his career he went to play for Wrexham. Tommy's brother Wally was also a fine player, and went to Carlisle. Some of the other Dock Star players earned caps for Wales while playing as amateurs.

These were only some of the players, and the list also included a goalkeeper called Charley Perring, a big man who could have gone a long way if he had had a mind to – or, at least, that's what the old gents told me. Jim Adams, my uncle was another who earned a cap, playing for the G.W.R.

football team – this was possible in those days. Other players included Trevor Pugh, brother of Tom Pugh, whose story follows, Gron Jones, John McCarthy, John Morgan, Johnny Morris, Reg Taylow and Johnny Coombes. Later on they set up the Dock Stars Juniors and these also turned out to be a fine team.

One outstanding character was Tom Pugh, a remarkable young footballer who lost his life while bravely trying to save three children from drowning. He and Charley Perring brought two in safely, went out for the third and disappeared, later being found drowned. He was a man of great courage and a devoted husband to his wife May, who was carrying his child at the time he died.

They also held greyhound racing on the Dock Stars ground – the hare was towed round the course by a bicycle wheel on a frame. People from all over the town came for a flutter, and later ended up in the Dock Hotel for a pint before going home to their loved ones. Often they would be singing their heads off as they went, but the old ones told me that there was no trouble; they all got together, arms around each other's shoulders, singing and laughing as they made their way home.

A lot of gambling went on in those days, and it was nothing to see a group of men standing around, playing pitch and toss, or perhaps gathered behind a bank, playing cards, with someone watching out for the police. Sometimes we boys would wander up to watch them, but often we would be swinging round a lamp post on ropes, or playing cat and mouse. This game was played with two sticks, one of them small and pointed at each end; we would flick at this with the other stick, trying to see who could hit it hardest. Meanwhile the girls would be playing hop-scotch on the pavement, or spinning their tops along, whipping them to see which one would keep going the longest.

If you go to Port Talbot docks today you will see that the Seamen's Mission is still standing; it is used now as the Sea Cadets headquarters. The Harbour House is also still standing, and opposite the Mission you can see the old lock entrance which was used before the new docks were built in the 1890s. The mission building was once part of the diphtheria hospital at Broom Hill, and was donated for its present purpose by the

Lions Club when the hospital closed. It was dismantled and rebuilt on the docks so that it could be used as a Seamen's Mission building.

At number one tip (coal tippler) was the Pilot's Rest inn, and the older people told me that Richard Burton's father lodged there while he was working on the docks, (he preferred to stay there rather than walk home to Pontrhydyfen every night). He had no idea in those days that he would become the father of a son who was to be one of the greatest Shakespearian actors in the world, a son whose voice was as smooth as a mountain stream, but who could roar like a waterfall, and who made Pontrhydyfen, a village that no one had heard of, into a place of world-wide fame. The Pilot's Rest (or 'Tiddlywink', as it was known) was built round about 1859, and the landlord at that time was Will Thomas (his relative, Dai Stephens, kept the paper shop in Tanygroes Street until very recently).

Coal, coke, patent fuel, tinplate and steel were exported from the docks, while imports consisted of copper, iron ore, pitwood and timber. The exports came chiefly from the Llynfi and Garw Valleys. Millions of tons of coal must have been exported from the docks during their active history, and the railways played an important part in handling the flow of exports and imports which went on for twenty-four hours a day. A very efficient scheme was worked out: railway wagons full of coal came from the Llynfi Valley in the morning and discharged their load onto the ship, then the same wagons went back to the Llynfi Valley, filled up again, returned to the docks and discharged these loads onto the same ship in the evening. I heard of this record-breaking system from an old weighman who noted the numbers of the wagons in the two shifts while he was working a doubler.

Chapter Two

I was six when the war broke out and I remember the men leaving to go to their regiments and later the women crying as their husbands and sons marched away. I soon realised what those tears meant, for my mother was informed that my father was missing after Dunkirk; later she was told that he was a prisoner of war. My mother was left with seven children to look after and she took a job in the melting shop. This was shift work, but our neighbours were wonderful people and we children were allocated to different houses in the street when she worked nights. The people of Dock Street made this possible, although some of them too had their husbands in the Forces.

We soon got used to the horrible sound of the warning siren, and our mother used to get us up when those sirens went, dress us and carry or drag us down to the railwaymen's air-raid shelter, which was down by the beach, in the sand tumps. We had to walk quite a distance over the railway sidings to get there, and it was only a small shelter. I remember how we would have to hurry there because those who were last couldn't get in. After the 'All Clear' we would tramp home again, where we would be put back to bed. Later on in the war they built us three air-raid shelters just outside our street.

I also remember a ship by the name of 'Stalheim', a Norwegian vessel, which left the dock last in a batch of four going out with the tide. Suddenly there was a big bang, and everybody ran down to the pier to see what had happened. We kids ran down there too, full of excitement, to find that the 'Stalheim' had hit a mine, just a couple of hundred yards off the pier. I believe there were six men killed, and for years the mast of the ship could clearly be seen sticking up in the sea. The pilot boat 'Marian Byass' which took her out was captained by Bert Gunn.

Another sight to be seen was Llandarcy oil works. It was bombed, and burned for over a week, and the black cloud of smoke that came from it could be seen clearly from where we sat on the sand tumps. We often climbed the tumps to look and see if the fire had gone out, and looking across the bay

11

we could also see clearly the barrage balloons over Swansea. There were so many of these that you might have thought that Swansea was being held up by them, especially after the bombing they had had.

Looking back now, I can see that we were very lucky, especially compared with what Swansea went through, though we *did* have to get used to the black-out warnings in the street. You would hear somebody shouting out 'Close those bloody curtains!' and going down the back garden to the toilet with a torch in your hand simply wasn't on. Instead you had to sit there in the dark, feeling for the toilet paper (cut-up squares from the *News of the World* or the *Daily Herald*) – all this after your brother took you down to the place, then left and ran like hell back into the house, leaving you crying out, 'I'm ready, I'm ready, I'm ready!'

Another sign of the war was to see everybody putting strips of brown sticky paper round the edges of their windows and across them, like crossword grids. Then some boy would come along and play OXO on your windows with chalk!

The first bombs to fall on the docks were dropped on August 17th, 1940; Army bomb disposal men arrived to defuse them.

One Saturday night in early 1941 we were just about to go to bed when our mother rushed us all under the stairs (the safest place if the house was bombed). We could hear a screaming noise coming down towards us, getting louder and louder, and I could hear my mother calling out that we were going to have it. She cwtched us all together. Then there was a terrible thud and the whole house shook, as though we were in an earthquake.

We could hear all the people running out of their houses and shouting that Number Six had been hit – but by some miracle the bomb never went off. Mr. and Mrs. Billy Williams and their children were under the stairs, only inches from where the bomb fell; it came right through their back kitchen. Mr. Williams scrambled the children out of the front door as quickly as possible, and the neighbours started to help them to safety.

Shortly afterwards the Dock Police arrived and the Army. They quickly began to evacuate the whole street. Within half an hour they had us marching in groups and we started off in the dark. Mr. and Mrs. Dai Williams and their son Willy helped my mother by taking my brother and me with them and I remember being carried on Mr. Williams's shoulder, while Mrs. Williams carried my brother. We began our journey by going under wagons, then crossing sidings and going up the embankment, and in the hurry we got separated from our family.

When we arrived at Phoenix Wharf the bombing was still going on, and the sky was flashing above us. Men ran out from the power house and hurried us inside, telling us that it was to dangerous to continue. They put us boys to sleep on a bed of bricks, but after an hour or two we were woken by the police; according to them, they had been all over the dock looking for us and trying to trace us by calling out our names on a loudspeaker. Eventually they took us by car to the Y.M.C.A. and on arriving there, we found our mother, who was relieved and happy to see us. All the people from the street were there too, sleeping on the floor.

A crowd of people had been in the Dock Hotel when word got to them that Dock Street had been bombed and those who were from the street ran like hell to get home. Some young girls had been up in town, dancing and they had a terrible shock when the Army would not allow them near the street. Many of the fathers had been working the afternoon shift.

Two boys – my brother Albert and Evett Thomas (of the family whose house had ben bombed) – had been in the Plaza Cinema when the bombing started. They went out and were rushed into the air-raid shelter opposite the cinema (where the Blue Star Garage is now). Then, after the 'All Clear', they decided to go home – but when they arrived at the street they found it deserted, so they agreed to sleep in Evett's house that night. They had not been there long when the police and the Army rushed them out again, so quickly that their feet didn't touch the ground, explaining to the boys that they were sleeping on top of an unexploded bomb. They looked at each other in shock, like angels in distress, then they were taken to the Y.M.C.A.

Memory is a strange thing. The one fact that stands out clearest in my mind today is that, being the last to arrive at

13

Y.M.C.A., we found that all the sweets had already been given out to the other children.

Although the bomb did not go off, one of Mr. Thomas's step-daughters, Jean (who was then three) still bears the scar of that day on her elbow, but she only remembers her father putting iodine on the wound as it bled. After the bombing she went to Bryn to live with relatives and has stayed there all her life, never returning to the street. (She is now Mrs. Jean Jones). Meanwhile we were all at the Y.M.C.A., and the next day my mother took some of us to relatives in Goytre; two of my brothers went to Velindre where Jim Adams, my mother's brother, lived. Some people had relatives in the country and Phyllis Evans took her family to Carmarthen to stay until it was safe to return, while others went to stay with relatives or friends around the town. Some even tried to go back to the street, but the Army would not let them in. (I think these people were worried about losing the coal in their shed). Meanwhile the Army defused the bomb and after a week we all returned home.

The month after all that was over, we were playing in the middle of the street, about eleven in the morning, when a plane came over. We all looked up and saw something dropping from it, then Mrs. Edna Pugh grabbed hold of me and rushed me behind the door of her house. Next thing there was a terrific explosion and when, after a couple of minutes, we all went out again, we saw, to our horror, that the German plane had bombed the Dock Stars football pitch, as well as hitting our only road to the street and knocking four or five railway wagons off a high bank. It also dropped one bomb through an engineering shop at the Baldwin's Margam Steelworks, which never went off and to make things even worse, it damaged the street's water supply, which meant that we had no running water and left a huge bomb hole in the middle of our access road. We had to fetch and carry our water from a long way off and we had to go out to meet the milk man and the baker's van every day for a week.

The Dock Police were very worried about the railway trucks that had been blown off the embankment. There was coal everywhere and they did their best to guard the hundreds of tons scattered all around, but in the night-time it slowly disappeared and every chimney in the street was smoking away happily!

After all this we were sure that Hitler had heard of Dock Street and sent Goering, his chief pilot, to bomb us. If so, he didn't do too badly (for the Germans, that is), hitting the street, hitting our only road, our water-pipes and our football pitch. He also set the warren on fire, and knocked the railway wagons full of coal off the embankment. We thought perhaps Hitler was angry because we still had so much coal even when he was sinking our coal ships.

At the bottom of the street we had the Army searchlight battery and at the top of the street we had a barrage balloon which was manned by the R.A.F. It was a great thrill to watch them putting the balloon up and then bringing it down again, using a winching machine; the R.A.F. men ran round busily while the corporal gave them their orders.

Sometimes, when I was a little boy, I would be woken by a commotion in the street when these R.A.F. men got into a fight with the local men. The R.A.F. men were billeted in one of Tom Keogh's fields with their balloon, but they used to go to the Dock Hotel, where the rows started and when the fight got going, it looked like Dodge City on a Saturday night.

There was a searchlight near the street too, manned by a crew of women and men, and we would often go over there to see them. They always chased us away though, perhaps because they thought we wanted to pinch their searchlight.

That Saturday night was just the beginning. One evening a German bomber started to drop incendiary bombs all round us and the men and the older boys ran to put the fires out. I can remember hearing some of the worried mothers crying out to their sons to come back but without success. All the warren was alight, and they kept damping down the fires for hours; it was the men and the big boys who put out the blaze and the boys became men overnight as they worked. As for us, our mothers had the task of stopping us from leaning out of the windows in our excitement, and getting us back to bed.

Then there was the time when workmen were cementing the stone pier and all of a sudden a German plane flew in from Swansea Bay, machine-gunning the pier right up to the lock gate and the docks. Men were running everywhere, like a storm of flies, but the plane turned off to its left, towards Baglan Mountain.

In order to bluff these German planes, big gun pits were dug between the stone pier and the Betsy Pool; large telegraph poles stuck out of these towards the sea, so that they looked like guns.

More excitement came to our street when some barrels of stout were washed up on our beach and men rushed down there from every house in the street. According to one story, certain men opened one of the barrels, to sample it, but went too far and got drunk. Then they buried one or two more barrels in the sand tumps – but they had drunk so much that the next day they could not remember where they had buried them. It seemed that some poor ship must have been sunk by the Germans, and the barrels it carried had ended up on our beach. Next day the customs officers came down and took the lot away, while the men looked on with stout running from their eyes.

These barrels were not the only things washed up on the beach. Some days timber props by the hundreds could be seen, and sometimes there were crates of oranges.

In 1943, when I was ten years old, a fleet of American ships arrived at Port Talbot Docks. With my friends from Dock Street, I watched them edge slowly through the narrow entrance of the lock gates with not an inch to spare. We were watching from a sand tump overlooking the locks because the Dock Police would not let us anywhere near the operation, but we could see the tanks and half-tracks loaded on the decks of the ships.

One by one the ships entered the docks and berthed, and within a matter of a day they had been unloaded by the overworked dockers and then loaded again onto low-loading railway wagons. The Great Western railwaymen wore dark uniforms and they stripped down to their waistcoats; shunters, loco drivers, checkers and weighmen all soon went into action, linking up the wagons which carried thousands of tons of military vehicles. Train after train left the docks on their way to a destination which I know now was southern England, and many a time I saw these locomotives struggle with the weight they were pulling, skidding and letting off steam as they went.

Row upon row of tanks and half-tracks lined the North Dock

(near where the Talbot Block Company's offices are today) and we boys, all very excited, often clambered up on them. Landing craft were welded together in sections at the dry dock, as were parts of the Mulberry Harbour which was to be used in the invasion of France. The dry dock workers carried out significant work in the build-up to the D-Day Normandy landings, but their contribution was not recognised, nor was that of the local dockers, railwaymen, Home Guard and Transport Police. Many of these men are now in their seventies and eighties, and can still tell stories of the vital part they played fifty years ago – but as far as the history books are concerned, only Swansea and Cardiff took part in the preparations for D-Day.

American soldiers also came, as well as ships and soon settled down in the area. They were camped at the Beach Hotel and in Hospital Road, while some took up residence at the Aberavon Rugby Ground. These last lived under the stand and parked their vehicles round the ground, and I remember that all hell was let loose when they found that one of their lorries had been set on fire. It was an accident, caused by some local boys mucking about and setting fire to the grass; the grass was wet with oil that had dripped from the various vehicles and it was soon blazing. The fire was soon dealt with by the Americans, but I wonder if those naughty boys still remember today the panic they caused.

The Americans also had a camp on the warren, near Dock Street; the tents were between No. 1 tippler and the stone pier opposite the lock gates. Our first meeting with these Yanks was one of those things that stick in one's memory for ever after. They called us youngsters over to give us chewing gum, but they were mainly negroes and we stood there amazed at the colour of their skins. We had seen coloured men coming off the ships in the docks, but standing here was an army of them. One railwayman said to another, 'Bloody Hell, they're black Yanks!' However they soon became friends, welcome in our close-knit community, and they went out of their way to please us. They gave us K-Rations and every child in the street learned to say 'Got any gum, chum?' At meal times they would have us children queuing up with them for ice cream which they collected in their mess tins. We used to play baseball with them too. One man, I remember, went by the name of Big Duke; he was a big man, a handsome negro, always over in our street.

We had chewing gum every day, and I can remember having six of the best with a cane, at school, when a teacher by the name of 'Daddy' Harris caught me chewing after a warning. It was like Christmas every day when the Yanks gave us sweets and chocolate, and I had my first cigarette at the age of eleven; it was a Camel. The older boys walked about like the American gangster actor George Raft with Chesterfield cigarettes hanging out of the sides of their mouths. We always hurried home from school to watch the soldiers training.

The Americans would come over to our street with their dirty washing and our mothers would wash and iron for them – the charge was 2/6 (two shillings and sixpence – 12½ pence) per bundle. It was handy for my mother, with seven children to keep and her husband a prisoner of war.

I remember sitting with the Americans in their tents on the sand tumps, talking about their homeland and the life they had there. They also told us how they were the grandchildren of the people who had been slaves in those terrible days of America's past. Their officers were white, and they were billeted at Phoenix Wharf, on the Junior Dock Stars football pitch. One of the officers, who became a good friend, used to talk about the ranch where he lived with his family, and before he left he gave me a musical instrument. I can't remember its name, but it was like an ostrich egg with holes in the side through which to play a tune; it was oval and smooth like a pebble. The Yanks also saved our silver threepenny pieces; they drilled holes in these and then made bracelets out of them, to take home for souvenirs or to wear round their own wrists. I often wonder how many of the bracelets that the veterans took back with them are still there in America today.

Their great joy was to be in the Dock Hotel drinking Truman's beer; many of them quickly discovered this beer and they named it 'firewater'. Sometimes they drank the place dry, and that made them unpopular with some of the dockers. There were often dances held at St. Joseph's hall on a Saturday night, and many fights occurred there too, with the local boys on leave; many fights also occurred between the black and white Yanks, at the bottom of Beach Hill (where the traffic lights are today). The local police and the American Military Police would go in to separate them, using pick handles, baseball bats and truncheons, then throw them into the backs of lorries to take them back to camp.

When we were in town on a Saturday, we would see the white Yanks going round in lorries, looking for local girls to take to the dances that they held at Margam Castle at the weekends. Many local girls fell in love with the soldiers (many of whom came from Pennsylvania) and in some cases they were so much in love that they married their sweethearts after the war. For instance, Miss Enid Harvey married Corporal Joseph Luke Cornell, Miss Kitty Ace married Warrant Officer David Thomas Jenkins and Miss Mary Ring married Sergeant George Fairley. Love blossomed for many in those dark days, between local girls and the 'overpaid, over here, chewing gum boys' from thousands of miles away.

The Americans staged mock landings at Morfa Beach, and it was said that the Supreme Commander General Eisenhower visited them at Margam Castle. Also Eisenhower and Montgomery drove through Jersey Marine before D-Day to boost the morale of the troops. I remember being at school when the whole town was covered by a smokescreen; we had to close all the windows and the incident was put down to the Americans training at Morfa Beach.

Nowadays people walking along Morfa Beach with metal detectors often find souvenirs such as cartridges and bullets, once used by the American and British soldiers who trained there. The R.A.F. also use Morfa as a practice area, towing old vehicles on to the beach as bombing targets; R.A.F. planes also towed targets across the bay so that the guns on the beach could practice firing.

In 1944, as the month of May came in, the Americans began to load up their ships at Port Talbot docks. Swansea Bay was covered with ships of all sizes – a sight such as I will never see again – and every gun and rocket launcher along the beach heads of Jersey Marine was alert and manned. Port Talbot, together with Swansea and Cardiff Docks, took an important part in the preparation for the D-Day invasion; they provided 150 vessels, carrying 89,371 tons of military stores and equipment, together with 41,630 personnel.

Our own Americans were part of the U.S. V Corps (2nd Division) and later they took part in the landings in France on D-Day Plus I and 2 (June 7th and 8th, 1944). One morning they had gone, as quietly as they had come, but I read in the Western Mail the year after that they had taken a serious battering at Omaha Beach.

The Americans were not our only unexpected visitors. One day we saw French liberty boats coming in to the lock. They were a horrific sight, with hundreds of wounded French soldiers all over their decks, and they were berthed at Margam Wharf, under the transporter. Everyone went down to see this terrifying sight, and the soldiers kept shouting down to us for bread. The men from the steelworks threw their sandwiches up to them and the soldiers threw rolls of French paper money back to us, and tins of meat as well. I remember how one man tried to catch a tin of meat, but it went through his hands, caught him on the forehead and split his head open.

This was on a Sunday, so we tried to buy some bread up town, going to Hooper's, the bakers, and Morgan's, but the only things we were able to get were Chelsea buns from Hooper's after we had knocked them up. So then we went back to the ships with our pockets bulging with French money, and three Chelsea buns – which we ate on the way. I don't know why these ships came in to the dock, because no-one was allowed to go onto them, and in a day or two they were gone.

Another time an American destroyer was towed in, in two halves. There were dead soldiers in one half, screened off by tarpaulins. I remember a frigate aground on Aberavon beach; this was during October 1944, and the ship had been torpedoed by a U-boat. There had been serious damage to her stern, and the weather was terrible that night, so the frigate landed on a sandbank. The Mumbles lifeboat took off her crew of 42 men, doing this with great courage and skill in the middle of the gale. Later I watched the frigate being towed into the dock by tugs; her stern was shattered. She was a Canadian ship by the name of H.M.S. Cheboque.

One day, late in 1944, we were told that something big had been washed up on the beach. We all ran down to see it and were quite out of breath when we arrived at the huge steel monster, but that didn't stop us from climbing on to it. Later we learned that it was part of the Mulberry Harbour used for D-Day. This section had broken off in a storm and had been washed up on the spot where once the Amazon ship had been wrecked. It stayed there for many years, and we used to swim in the pool that was left inside it when the tide went out. In the end it was broken up.

One Sunday morning we boys were playing football not far from the lock gates when a single engined aeroplane swooped down over us. It dived behind a large sand tump, down towards the beach, and didn't come up again, so we all ran to the top of the tump. From there we could see that it had landed by the stone pier; it was at the water's edge.

With much excitement we all ran to it, meeting the pilot on the way down. He told us that he had been forced to land because of engine trouble but on landing, the plane had hit a steel post and punctured one of its wheels. (These steel posts were planted all over the beach, to stop any German planes landing). The pilot had a trainee with him and we told them that the tide was on the turn and would soon be coming in. At that the pilot went to the docks to telephone for help, while we boys and the trainee picked the plane up from behind and turned it towards the beach. We pushed the plane right up to the pebbles near the Round House, but it was difficult to push because of the puncture.

In the meantime Garnet Morgan and Albert Parsons had come down to give us a hand. The only way we could push the plane was to put a couple of the boys on the wing opposite to the punctured wheel and then heave, but as we could not leave it where it was, we all pushed and pushed until eventually we got it to the Betsy Pool, a quarter of a mile away. We puffed our lungs out with the effort, but at last we left the plane on a sandbank.

While this was going on, our mothers provided refreshments for the pilot and his trainee. Then the R.A.F. engineers arrived, and by the end of the evening they had repaired the machine. By then the tide had come in and gone out again, so the pilot and the trainee got into the plane and taxied it down, ready for take off, giving some of us a ride on its wings as they went. Then, with a wave from the pilot, it took off and we all cheered. Later on an R.A.F. officer came specially to thank us, and our hard work was also mentioned in the papers.

We discovered later on that the aircraft had been on a routine training flight from R.A.F. Brawdy, near Haverfordwest. Curiously enough, the pilot was a Port Talbot boy, Kenneth Barrass, who had been born at Waterfall Cottages, Taibach; at the time of this incident, his family was living in Pen-y-Cae Road. I learned this some years later, from a very good friend of his, Jack Purchase, who had also been a pilot during the war. Jack Purchase also told me that Kenneth Barrass had been on active service in the Far East and when the Japanese surrendered in 1945, he was the Commanding Officer of a small group of R.A.F. personnel then being held by the Japanese; it was his duty to accept the sword of the Japanese commanding officer as a token of their surrender to the Allied Forces. In 1950 Kenneth Barrass emigrated to Canada where he is still living.

One day, in the middle of the war, my mother had the surprise of her life when she opened a letter and found a cheque for one hundred pounds. This was from the family of Gordon Rolls, who was a prisoner of war with my father, and it was in thanks for my father saving their son's life.

It seemed that the two of them had been on a death march together, from Poland to Germany, in appalling conditions. Thousands of British prisoners had tramped through blizzards and those who fell out were left by the roadside to freeze to death or were bayoneted in the back. This I think, was when my father saved Gordon Rolls, carrying him on and on, and I remember him saying when he got home that he had had a pal who was a millionaire's son. It seemed that Gordon Rolls had asked if he could send some money to my father's family and my father had told him to send a hundred pounds, thinking, of course, that he was pulling his leg.

In the meantime my mother had so much money that she did not know what to do with it – though we all had new shoes. My eldest brothers helped her to spend it and kept a check on her, because a hundred pounds was worth several thousand pounds today. One other thing I will always remember is my father coming home from the war and finding that his army gratuity was going to be taxed. It was a disappointment that he shared with thousands of other British servicemen who had been through the war, and it made him wonder if it had been worth it; he was never the same man who had gone off to France to defend his country.

We must not forget, either, the part played by the women of Port Talbot. Hundreds were employed in the tinplate industry, at the Borough, Ffrwydwyllt, Mansel and Guest, Keen and Baldwin's works and though they are in their seventies and eighties now, they still bear the scars of that work on their arms and legs. As workers, they were fully on a level with the rollermen and doublers. I worked at the Borough Tinplate Works before I went into the army and I can bear witness that they were the backbone of the industry, with turbans round their hair, and aprons and gloves. I was a blacksmith's striker to Gwilym Williams, the blacksmith who made the tongs with which the doublers gripped the sheets as they were flung across the room to double them. Every pair of tongs had to be perfect, because if one broke, a man could have his leg cut off by the flying sheet; but Gwilym was very reliable.

Young or old, married or single, these hundreds of women went home dirty and sweaty every night. It was especially hard for those married women whose husbands were at war and who had a houseful of children to look after. Their shift started again as soon as they got home and they were washing and scrubbing clothes – by hand in the sink, with a tub and a scrubbing board, then ironing and cleaning. They were truly women of steel, with no leisure, only much work and little sleep. Many worked on the railways and also took part in the A.R.P. or Home Guard. Others went away to factories or to the Land Army and quite a few caught packed trains to Bridgend to work at the arsenal there, manufacturing bombs and shells. The W.R.A.F. (Women's Royal Air Force) were stationed at the docks, on searchlights, barrage balloons and the ack-ack guns. All these were the so-called weaker sex.

Some of the young girls from the town worked at the Wern, Briton Ferry and they caught their buses from the Bethany Square bus stop. Another forgotten army who also used the stop by the level crossing at Bethany was the Bevin Boys, drafted into the mines; they worked down in those godforsaken black holes, bringing up thousands of tons of the coal needed for the war effort. But even then those men, marked with blue scars on their faces, were not given the credit they deserved. I remember seeing them coming home after their shift, as black as when they left the pit head – too black to mix with the rest of the passengers sitting on the Thomas Bros. bus. They would have to stand on the bottom of the steps at the entrance of the bus, and I have even seen people so bloody-minded that they swore about the miners being on the bus in that state. At the time I thought to myself that those who complained would be the first to grumble if there was no coal to warm them. The miners worked at the Newlands, Glenhafod, Bryn and Cynon Vale collieries.

Great excitement came to our street when we learned that the war was over. My mother was especially delighted because my father had been a prisoner for five years and the whole street prepared to welcome him home. They painted 'Welcome Home Ernie' in large letters on the walls of the air-raid shelter – but then one day he arrived home quite unexpectedly.

I was in the house with my mother, sister and brothers when somebody rushed in and said, 'Ernie's home!' We went out and saw everyone rushing to greet my father; then we saw this small, thin, little man in brown, hurrying towards us. The house was packed all day with people coming in and out, some crying because they knew *their* sons wouldn't be coming home.

One by one the rest of the fathers came home. My brother Verdun came back a month after my father's return and it was a wonderful occasion, standing in our back garden with my mother and my brothers, Jimmy, Richard and Raymond, and watching my mother as she saw her oldest son embracing his father after five years absence. Tears were running down their faces. (Verdun had joined the Royal Navy by cheating on his age; he served on the MTBs [Motor Torpedo Boats] in Sicily).

When the official announcement that the war had ended came through, every boat in the dock blew its hooter, as did the dry dock, the Steelworks, the tinplate works up in town (Borough, Mansel and Ffrwdwyllt) and all the locomotives (which also let off steam all round our street). They were blowing off their hooters in sheer delight at the good news.

After that, celebrations went on all over the town. Aberavon Beach was illuminated in the evening and the members of the British Legion held parties for their children at the Y.M.C.A. One of the main events of the rejoicings was a service held at Wesley Hall, conducted by the Rev. E. Whitford Roberts, with Mr. F.L. Thomas reading the lesson. As for V.E. Day, there were events all over the borough: at Wesley Church, Cwmavon, the children were treated to a tea party they will always remember; in Prior Street there was dancing and the forecourt walls, without their railings due to the war effort, served as seats for those who wanted to watch the dancing; at Wern Road, Margam, there was a tea party, with sports and later on dancing round a bonfire; the tea party at Richard Street, Aberavon, was opened by Flying Officer Percy James, who had been born in the street; and at the Plaza Cinema, the Royal Artillery (Portsmouth) gave an orchestral concert – the band stretched right across the stage and gave a performance that brought the house down! In the week that the war in Europe came to an end, the Regent Cinema was showing Boris Karloff in 'The Climax', the Grand Cinema had Mervyn Johns in 'Twilight Hour', and the Majestic Cinema showed Gene Tierney in 'Laura'.

Once the Germans had surrendered, the V1 and V2 bombs no longer fell on London and the evacuees began to move back home from Port Talbot. These young 'invaders' had come to us from London for safety nearly five years before and now they stood on the station with their adopted 'parents', excited to be going home, but also sad to be leaving these people who had cared for them. The mayor of Port Talbot, Councillor Mrs. L.C. Edwards, J.P., came to see the evacuees off.

Councillor Mrs. Edwards also joined the V.E. Day thanksgiving parade from the Memorial Park to St. Mary's Church. This was headed by the bands from Briton Ferry and Pontrhydyfen, with units from the R.A.F., while the Mayor and her guests were also there, and hundreds of people watched the procession. However, the most popular place at that time was Port Talbot Railway Station, where kit bags fell to the floor unnoticed as their owners wrapped their arms around their loved ones.

Now that the war was over, the brown sticky paper was taken

off the windows and the blackout came down. Then German prisoners arrived, to take down all the barbed wire fencing. We went down into the sand dunes to see them, expecting to find big, strong, blonde monsters, only to discover that they were much like us.

Chapter Three

The people of Dock Street were not wicked, but there was more than one occasion when coal got them into trouble. The Thirties and Forties were times of great poverty and when we were surrounded with sidings filled with coal wagons and needed coal in order to survive the wild winters, it was inevitable that we would play Robin Hood from time to time.

We very rarely had coalmen delivering in the street, so we would take 'samples' from the coal wagons. What a sight it was to see a locomotive pulling these wagons down towards the street! The loco would be puffing, skidding up the incline towards the top of the street, then somebody would call out 'Engine coming!' and all of a sudden people would drop everything and run towards the train. They would jump on the trains while they were still in motion – it was like Indians attacking a wagon train in a cowboy film. Then they would stand on top of the wagon until it reached their backgates (which were up against the embankment) when they would throw the coal down the bank so that it rolled up against the gates. This was done in a minute or two, then out came the brooms, and the lane was swept clean as if nothing had happened by the time the Dock Police arrived.

While this was going on, the locomotive driver and his shunters didn't know what to do – laugh or cry! Some would try to throw us off by braking suddenly, but we would not move. Sometimes we even used to grease the rails to slow the loco down; and we always put someone (often the youngest boy) on top of the embankment overlooking the dock to make sure the police bicycle brigade was not coming.

Sometimes the Dock Police would hide either behind some of the wagons or behind one of the railway workers' cabins, and when they saw us, they would blow their whistles. At that we would drop everything and run like the wind back to our houses, hiding behind locked doors as the policeman patrolled up and down the street. He would have his bike with him, because past experience told him that if he left it behind when he gave chase, he would never see it again.

At other times the men would put their wives on to the coal

wagons, unhitch the wagons and let them roll towards the street. Then the men would brake the wagons and the women would throw the coal down, after which the men put the lovely big lumps into their coalhouses and swept up any evidence. After that the men helped their wives down off the railway wagon, saying, 'Well done, my love.' Some of the women could climb up those wagons like mountaineers, but the cleverness of it all was that if they got caught, it was the women who were summonsed, not the men. The men left as soon as the police came in sight.

Some of the women got caught on top of the wagons, but some picked up their skirts and ran like hell. As one policeman said, 'You couldn't see their backsides for dust', and being clever, they always ran to the front of the street. The police chasing them would be on the railway bank behind the street, and when they arrived at the front everything would be as normal. The policemen would walk up and down the street, looking for anything out of place, while one woman pretended to scrub her doorstep with no water and another would be pretending to clean her windows with her husband's best underpants. Some would be hiding behind moving curtains, sweating.

There was one dock policeman we all knew very well; he was fair, but sometimes he could be a real pain because he knew every move we made. Sometimes we would see him coming down a low level siding on his bike; he would leave it under the bridge that went out over the sidings and then he would patrol the sidings. As soon as he was out of sight, we would get hold of the bike, tie a rope round it and pull it up from the top of the bridge, leaving it dangling in mid-air. Later he would come back, take his helmet off and stand scratching his head, muttering under his breath as he looked at the bike dangling above him. He was George Davies, a real policeman.

There was one funny story about four boys going out to pinch coal on a bitter winter night, taking their dog with them. They walked along the track, avoiding bumping into telegraph poles in the dark, until they reached the wagons, climbed up and began filling their sacks. Then the dog, down on the ground, made a noise, half bark, half scream and ran like hell. They looked up the track as the moon came out and saw someone peddling his bike towards them like a charging bull with its head down. They threw their half-filled sacks down to the ground, jumped down and ran like the clappers.

As they ran away, they heard a crash and a yell, and the boys looked at each other and burst out laughing. They stopped, and one said to the others, 'He must have run into our sacks!' Then they began to run again and jumped down the bank in the dark – only to find themselves up to their waists in water in a bog. They stayed there for a while, until it was all clear, then went home, soaking and freezing. From that day on they never knew if it had been a policeman or a railwayman on the bike.

As they approached the street, you could hear their feet swishing about in their waterlogged shoes; and as the four reached Johnny Coombes's house at the end of the street they saw their little dog sitting on the doorstep, waggling his tail as if to say 'You've been a long time!'

On another occasion a man was caught standing on top of a coal wagon with a lump of coal in his hand. Along came a sergeant in the Dock Police, who stood below him and told him to drop what he was holding and come down. The man obliged – and the lump of coal dropped right on top of the sergeant's head, knocking him out. The man ran like hell!

I will always remember one lady, climbing up an embankment on her way home to the street. She had a shawl wrapped round her, Welsh fashion, as if she was carrying a baby. On the top of the bank stood a railway policeman, leaning on his bike, who held out his hand to assist her. 'I can manage,' she said, then, as she was passing him, the policeman said, 'It's a cold day, I see you've got him well wrapped up and warm.' 'Yes,' she said, 'he's fast asleep,' and she walked past the man and down the other side of the embankment towards her back gate. Once there, she opened her coalhouse door and took a beautiful lump of coal out of her shawl. It was a beauty!

We weren't always so lucky. One beautiful morning, with the sun shining through the parlour window, Madeline Haines and Lil Willment tapped on our window and came in. They told my mother, Eva, that there was some coal up on the bank, spilled out of the railway wagons while they were shunting just behind our house. The three of them took their dustpans and went up the bank, where they bent down and began to fill the pans. Then Mrs. Willment, who was on her knees behind Madeline and my mother, saw silver buttons glittering in front of her eyes; she said a quick prayer and shouted 'Oh my God, no!' My mother and Madeline turned around and saw Jim 'Trigger' Davies, a dock policeman, standing there like a telegraph post.

Their mouths were still open when he said, 'Come on, get up and give me your names.' Mrs. Willment was terrified when he put his hand on her shoulder, and she said, 'Let us off, my husband works on the railway, he'll get the sack – and it's only a bit of coal that fell off the wagon.'

However the policeman took their names and reported them. A week went by, and then the summonses arrived. The three put on their Sunday best to face the magistrates in court, and the court was packed to the door. They stood there like Christians ready to be thrown to the lions; my mother Eva, a big, strong-looking woman; Madeline, slight and looking as if she didn't have a care in the world; and little Lil, shaking like a leaf. Lil whispered to Madeline, nodding at the Bench, 'They look like bloody bald parrots.' Behind them stood Sergeant Dando, a big man with a pot, giggling at what Lil had said, and later she told us that she could feel his stomach vibrating as he giggled.

The court stood in silence as the charge was called out. 'How do you plead?' asked the magistrate. 'Not guilty,' replied Eva in a deep voice. 'Not guilty,' Madeline replied, looking at the floor. Lil whispered so quietly that the magistrate shouted, 'Speak up!' and Lil, shocked, yelled back, 'NOT GUILTY!' Then they read the fines out: Eva Parsons, fined £1; Madeline Haines, fined £1; Lil Willment, fined fifty shillings, first offence. The three went home to pick dewberries and sell them to pay the fines. Mrs. Willment's husband kept his job.

We boys had many kicks up the backside or clips on the ear from the various policemen when we were caught in trouble, and if we told our parents, we would get the same from them. (Sadly, things have changed today).

Even apart from the coal, the railway was important in our lives. In order to go shopping, our mother had to climb the railway embankment, bend to go under railway wagons and go down a rail siding. There were three ways to get from Dock Street to town: one was by crossing the lock gates, then walking up the tram road to the Halfpenny Bridge; another was to cross the dock by launch near the Rio Tinto (that way you come out by the station); and the third was through the works (Thomas, Keen and Baldwin) and on under the transporter, this way ending up in West End Street, Taibach. Whichever way one went, it was two miles journey.

We kids learned to bend under the wagons before we could walk. On a rough day, too, the launch would bounce up and down and it took some doing when our mothers tried to jump on board with bags of shopping! They would wait until the boat rose up and then jump on. The launch crossing cost one penny.

One woman, by the name of Mag Evans, was crossing underneath an empty railway wagon in the low level sidings, meaning to go to the town, when all of a sudden the wagon moved off, dragging her along with it. It was only thanks to the alertness of the shunter, who heard her scream, that the loco was stopped. The railwaymen ran back and found her lying underneath the wagon; they rushed her to hospital where she had her big toe off. The same woman missed the lock gate and fell into the lock twice; she always hung on to her purse. They said she was like a cat with nine lives.

I can still remember some of the railwaymen – shunters, engine drivers and foremen, people like Len Williams, Ramsey Sweeney, Dai Nettles, Walter Woods, Jack Matthews, Cyril Charles and Roy Blackwell. (And they too still have tales to tell of those days, tales to make their audience laugh its head off). We boys used to play a game of walking on the railway lines to see who could get furthest before falling off; we would always leap-frog over the points every time we saw a set, but many failed the test and hopped home like a kangaroo, in agony.

Sometimes, when women went out with their prams, they would come across coal on the ground, lumps which had either fallen off the wagons while they were being shunted or had been left there deliberately to be collected. The woman would pick up her baby, put the coal in the bottom of the pram, cover it with a blanket, then put the baby back on top and walk away, with the baby crying its lungs out because of the lumps of coal sticking up its bottom. I don't think anybody got caught this way – but it must have been heavy going, pushing the pram home!

My mother's best friend was Verna Crealock (she later became Mrs. Johnny Brennan) and she was a woman full of life who could run like a hare. One day Verna, two sisters from the street and myself were in an empty wagon, scraping the sides for coal when a head popped over to look into the wagon. The four of us glanced up and saw a policeman's helment; the man put his hand on Verna's shoulder and said he had caught us. To my surprise the two sisters flew out of the coal wagon before me, and all I could see was the two women running ahead of me, holding their skirts up, with a cloud of dust trailing behind them.

Poor Verna got summonsed because the policeman had held her by the shoulders as he watched three clouds of dust running like hell. She later appeared before the magistrate, who turned out to be Williams, Cloth Hall, but before she went to Court she paid a visit to Billy Thomas at number six. He advised her what to say and it paid off; she got off with a caution and had to pay five shillings costs. We helped her with the fine.

We became experts on coal. The coal came shunting down to us and we could tell by the labels which was the best; we were trained to recognise which was good and which was anthracite (fool's coal).

What baffled us was that the Dock Police, who had control boxes on every entrance leading to the docks, had coal fires in these boxes, and to get coal they took it off the wagons. Nothing was done about them helping themselves; they had to keep warm, I suppose, like everybody else.

Chapter Four

There were some wonderful characters in the street. One was old man Willment who would take us boys and girls on walks with him. He was a pipe-smoker and we would collect dock leaves for him, then he would dry them and roll them in the palm of his hand until the leaves looked like tobacco. Next he would put them in the oven beside the fireplace to dry. His daughter was always finding them when she was working and she would play hell with him till he got them out, because she wanted to use the oven. Sometimes we would sit on the pavement listening to the old man's tales.

Then there was Dai Williams who lived at number one. We used to tease him by playing postman's knock; we would tie a length of cotton to his knocker, then we would hid behind the air-raid shelter and pull the cotton string until the knocker started to knock on the door. We would repeat this a couple of times until he caught on and chased us around the street. He would end up by going to our fathers, who would either give us a clip round the ear or make us stay in. Later we learned that Dai had been an old soldier who was a hero in the First World War. He had been badly injured and had a silver plate in his head because of these injuries. It shocks me now to think that we used to tease him. During the war he used to patrol the street at night and it was he who carried me on his shoulder on the awful night of the bombing.

Dai and Will Evans were brothers and used to swim from the pier to Morfa Beach. They were very good strong swimmers and the best pair I have ever seen for swimming under water. We used to sit on the beach, watching them and wondering where they were going to pop up. We also used to go dragging a fish net along the shore with them; one of them would be out in the water up to his shoulder and the other would be close to the shore. Then they would drag the net the full length of the beach. Afterwards they would give us a try, and by the end our arms would feel as if they were dropping off.

There was Tom Keogh, too, who ran a small farm outside the street, a strict man with a large family; he had daughters and one boy, the youngest child, whose na

John. He was religious too and if you were up early on a Sunday morning, you could see him taking his family to church and back. Tom Keogh was a strong-minded man and he farmed all the surrounding fields, which he fenced in. His daughters helped him on his farm, but he was very possessive, and if he saw us walking in his fields he would say, 'Get off me land!' I think if he could have fenced us in like his horses and cows, he would have been happy.

Once some of Tom Keogh's cattle drifted on to the railway lines and a train full of coal came around the bend and ran over them. I believe six cows were killed and I watched the plate-layers going to the rescue with the rail gangs.

Garnet Morgan had accidentally shot his foot during the war, and he went around with a bit of a limp. He had a shed on his allotment and kept birds there. He had all sorts of birds, from canaries to finches and he caught linnnets and finches with a net at the end of his allotment and bred them. People played cards there too, and I believe he must have trained his birds to read our hands and tell him what we had by the way they went 'tweet, tweet'! Garnet and my brother Albert were good friends, and went shooting ducks together down at the Betsy Pool.

Another wonderful character was Johnny Brennan. He would organise a carnival, and got us to dress up for Whitsun, then paraded us round the street. He always dressed up as a schoolboy, with shirt out, stockings down and mustard down the back of his legs, running from his trousers, and he would have the street in stitches. Then the women would bring out the tables and put them in the middle of the street, filling them with cake, trifle and sandwiches.

Billy Thomas who lived at number six Dock Street was our 'Perry Mason'. He had the intelligence of a lawyer and he was the man whom everyone went to for advice when they were in trouble; he would also write letters on their behalf when needed. Billy was a small man, with a large family to support, and he worked in a signal box on the Rhondda and Swansea Bay Railway; his box was by the tramroad, opposite the waterfalls on the river Afan. He was always ready to help others – with the exception of the Dock Police, and was a man of wit and understanding.

There was one famous story about how he was caught with coal in his possession. The police locked and sealed his coalhouse securely with their own padlock and went away to get a lorry in which to carry off the evidence. When they came back, they went to the coalhouse door, which had not been tampered with; the padlock, too, was fast shut. But when they opened the door, they went red as beetroot – the coalhouse was completely empty, the walls were whitewashed and the floor was so clean you could have eaten off it. The police ranted and raved, but Billy Thomas just stood there, calm and innocent, wanting to know what all the fuss was about; he got off for lack of evidence! There were several different stories told about this, but according to his son, he had taken every slate off the roof of the coalhouse, jumped inside, taken every lump of coal out and put it back into the coalwagon, then whitewashed the walls and swept up every bit of coal dust. Finally he put every slate back into place as if nothing had ever happened.

Harry and Florrie Clarke lived at number three. Harry worked on the railway, at Dyffryn Yard, and was a hard-working man and a likeable fellow, while his wife, Florrie, was the heart and soul of the street. When we had street parties, she would dress up in fancy clothes; she would take the curtains from her windows and wrap them around herself, then she would make a big fancy hat, decorated with whatever she could lay her hands on and sew on to the hat shape. There would be roars of laughter as she came out of her house, and she would follow this up by wiggling her hips and singing like Carmen Miranda, the American film star. Florrie was never in, she was always out enjoying herself in the street.

There were many others that I remember too – Mrs. Coombes, who lived next door to us, a wonderful old lady; old Mrs. Tooze, a little woman; and Mrs. Mag Evans, excitable and hard-working. Then there was Mrs. Haines from number twenty-three who lost a son at sea during the war. He was reported missing, believed drowned, after his boat went down, but she hoped and prayed all through the war that he would come home. Mrs. Crealock's son also died early in the war, and Mrs. McCarthy's son was lost on the same convoy as Mrs. Haines's boy; both boys were seventeen years old.

The Deare sisters, Cassy and Beryl, were a happy-go-lucky pair, the life and soul of many a party. They would come from the Dock Hotel singing together as if they had no worries in the world and they would cross the ballast on the embankment carrolling away like skylarks in the skies. Then they would cross the railway lines, carefully picking their feet up so that they stepped over the rails onto the sleepers; if the sleepers were wet, they were very slippery and you could slide like Bambi on ice. After crossing the lines they would go, still singing, down the bank opposite their back gate; the bank was very steep and they would try to walk down very carefully, but from about the middle they automatically had to run the rest of the way down. You could hear them screaming as they flew through their gate, ending up laughing and out of breath, and Cassy would put her finger to her lips, shushing her sister and saying, 'We'll wake the street!' They were wonderful singers, as was their other sister, Marian.

The embankment behind the street was very high and steep and difficult to climb, especially when it had been raining. Sometimes you would get half-way up, then you would slide down and have to start all over again, and sometimes our mothers, climbing down with their shopping, would end up on their backsides, holding up their shopping bags in front of them. We would run to help them, trying to control our laughter, and take the shopping bags out of their hands, because in there were the grub and the week's comics. As for our mothers, they had to help themselves up!

After all the years we lived there, nobody ever tried to make steps up the bank so that it would be easier for us. Many a pair of knickers were blackened going up or down that bank.

Next door to us lived an ex-carnival queen, Betty Davies, a blonde beauty. She used to bike to work every morning and when she passed the steelworks (Guest, Keen and Baldwin) men would run out to watch her and whistle. As a young lad, innocent as I was, I thought they had come out to have a look at her bicycle frame. Her father was an expert gardener, with a greenhouse and every year this glasshouse would be filled with the grapes he had grown. There were many temptations when I looked over the wall, but he kept his treasures firmly locked up.

I think there were only two proud owners of cars in the street. One was Ken Pugh, who lived at number nine with his wife Edna and three daughters and a son; he had to lock it away on his allotment because of the petrol shortage and later on he sold his pride and joy – though he regretted it.

The other car owner was our next door neighbour at number twenty, Betty's father, Morris Davies. Before the war Mr. Davies had loved motor bikes and now his car was polished lovingly and garaged every time it rained. Apart from Betty, his family included his wife Kitty, his other daughters Joyce and Lorraine (who in later years became a school teacher and then a head-mistress), and his son Morris. Morris served in the Royal Navy during the war, and after his ship went down, he was in an open boat for a week before being picked up.

Mr. Davies worked on the railway all his life and ended his career in the main signal box at Port Talbot station. He cycled to work every day on his old bike and a couple of the older boys played a trick on him once when he was coming home in the dark after an afternoon shift. The boys found a tailor's dummy on the old town tip and they waited until he was in sight, then put the naked dummy in the middle of the road. So there was Mr. Davies, peddling away like hell in the dark; he hit the dummy, went flying through the air like a shunting pole and landed in a ditch. He got up, still dazed, and went back into the road where he found what he thought was this naked lady. Then all you could hear was, 'Oh my God, what have I done?' as he repeated it over and over again. At last he picked up his bike, put it over his shoulder and ran away at top speed, still thinking he had knocked down a naked woman.

Old Mr. Crealock was a very good handyman. He made a lot of his own furniture with driftwood from the beach and any other pieces of wood he could find lying about. Among other things he made a Welsh dresser for his grand-daughter and this was so good that, after seeing it, people asked him to make one for their daughters. At Christmas time especially he would make toys out of wood; he was a very likeable man.

Perhaps the final place in this account of the characters of Dock Street should go to our most distinguished ex-resident. Lord Heycock once lived in Dock Street, when he was a little lad. He lived there with his aunt, and according to Rachel Crealock (as she was then) this was at number four. (Rachel herself was eighty-odd and looking like a spring chicken when she told her sister Verna).

I feel it was an honour to be born in the same street where he once lived, though it was before my time. He was a man of outstanding calmness, a caring loving family man, someone who aimed for the top and got there. Llewellyn Heycock gave up much of his own precious time to union matters and education – not forgetting Aberavon Rugby Club, of which he was President for many years. He went from the footplate of a locomotive to an honoured place in society, an achievement which no other man in Port Talbot has equalled.

From a railwayman to a lord,
A man who loved his God,
A loveable family man
Who became an Aberavon fan.

On a footplate he would stand
Planning ahead a promised land,
A man who built up steam,
A man who lived for his dream.

A Taibach man at heart,
His personality became an art;
School education became his life,
Along with his lovely wife.

Strong as a Welshman,
He became a nobleman.
His memory lives on today
Like the sun giving out a ray.

Chapter Five

Our house had three bedrooms up and two rooms down, with a back kitchen. There were nine of us altogether, so five of us boys slept in one bed, three of us up the top of the bed and two of us down the bottom. Two of my big brothers slept in the second room, and my father, my mother and our baby sister slept in the other one. In those black and wintry days there was no hot water, so getting up to wash was like trying to put a dog out in the snow. We would all be scrambling round the fire, warming our backsides, until our mother moved us so that she could do the toasting; she did this in twos, with a toasting fork about six inches long, holding the toast toward the fire, just an inch or two away from the bars until it was nice and brown.

Then we would sit around an old wooden table with a really posh tablecloth – four sheets from a newspaper, the Daily Sketch – eating our thick slices of toast with jam on them (instead of butter, which had run out because of the rationing) and a mug of tea so strong that the spoon stood straight up in it. There would be jam or marmalade in the tea instead of sugar, because of the rationing; and we had good old chips and spam for many a dinner time.

Everything was rationed during the war and for some years after: meat, butter, tea, sugar, clothing etc. The only things they didn't ration were the rabbits and dewberries, so out we would go with the dogs and try to chase the rabbits on the beach. Sometimes they would head for the water until the dog caught them at water's edge. Sunday dinner became 'Rabbit in the Ruff', followed by dewberry pie or stewed dewberries and custard, with the dog sitting staring up by the side of the table, waiting for his share. (After all, he had caught it). He would take his share of the rabbit back under the table, always keeping an eye on the cat, which was ready to pounce the minute he took a breather.

Even if our mother put all our meat coupons together, she would only have enough for a joint at the end of the week, so a lot of coupon swapping went on. We had powdered egg (dried egg), but if you ate too much of that either it would eat you or you would have to run for cover. Bread pudding was made for tea times, but the problem was playing football after eating it; you felt too heavy to run, so everybody wanted to play in goal.

Some of us in the street did not have much in the way of luxury, especially those from large families. They would go to school with holes in their shoes and patches on the backside of their trousers; in my case and those of others like me, I would wear the shoes one day and my brother wore them the next day. (We used to take labels off the coal wagons on the railway and use them to cover the holes in our shoes). We unfortunate kids would be stared at and pointed at by other children: 'Look at him with a hole in his arse!' came the comment many a time – and many a time it ended in fighting in the school yard.

Those children with shining black boots, creases in their trousers and their mammy bringing them to school, had their fathers working on the railways or in the tinworks, the docks or the steelworks, with a pay-packet coming in every week. It was not so for us Cinderellas who were part of a large family and had our fathers in the war, fighting; we had not seen them for years.

Even some of the teachers at school ignored us when we came to school in the rain; we would be dripping right through and made to sit apart from the rest until the clothes dried on us. Those bloody-minded teachers did not realise that most of us walked three miles to school, like the Goytre children. I can see one teacher now, shaking his head and muttering to himself and pointing to a corner, saying 'Go and stand over there until you've dried out.'

When dinner time came, we had dried out. Some went back home for dinner but most of us stayed and opened our sandwiches. These were damp with the rain and wrapped in pages from the News of the World, and consisted of bread and jam or dripping sandwiches. They were so thick that if you dropped one and it landed on your foot, it would bruise your toe. Then there was good old bread pudding (Dock Street wedding cake) for afters. After that we would climb the school wall to get some Spanish root to suck, or buy a red hot loaf of bread from Hooper's, the baker's. There were no free meals then in school; the only thing that was free was the milk, which we put on the radiators to warm, to stop us shivering after coming to school soaked through.

It was hard times for the girls too when they went to school, but they were hard as nails and could look after themselves. The only time we looked after them was when they either went dancing or to the pictures; then we would go and meet them by the lock gates, bring them across the warren, through the sidings, up over the embankment and into the street. Brothers would meet their sisters because it was very dark and a lot of foreign sailors were about the docks. After all, our Dock Street girls were the prettiest in town!

Many times my mother went to see the Means Test officials to try to get some extra money to help her through hard times during the war years. I remember her waiting all the morning with my brother Raymond, seven years old, and myself, nine years old, while we watched her plead for a couple of shillings to help her through her difficulties. They would ask her if she had got this or that in our home and tell her that if she did have these things she could sell them and get some extra cash.

We had gone with her to show them that we needed shoes, and in the end she came away with two shillings and sixpence (12½p). Looking back, I still remember all the women there queuing up with their children and having to beg. To make things worse, most of these women, like our mother, had their husbands in the Forces. My mother neither smoked nor drank.

There were a lot of big families in the street. Johnny Coombes lost his wife and brought up eight children, with the eldest, Dorrian, aged about fourteen years old, taking on the role of mother to them; the youngest was a baby boy called Richard. In fact, what with the Keoghs, the Crealocks, the Pughs, the Evanses, Morgans, Jenkinses and Willments, there were so many children that you could have filled as many as twenty-five railway wagons – the dogs would have filled the guard's van.

Our own family was nine, including my parents. My mother had hardly seen us as youngsters because she had had to see to everything after my father was taken prisoner at St. Valery during the Dunkirk campaign. My sister Ceinwen was the youngest of us, born just before my father was captured – if the war had not begun, we might have had a soccer team.

In the early nineteen fifties four of us were in the Army at about the same time: Jimmy, Richard, Raymond and myself; we were all Regulars except for Raymond, who was a National Serviceman. Of my other two brothers, Verdun was in the Navy and Albert in the Army, but they had completed their service; Mother Nature caught up with them and they got married. This was c.1952.

I cannot remember anyone being seriously ill in Dock Street. Everybody seemed to be fit and well, especially if they had been born there, and we all lived off the land and had the benefit of fresh air blowing from the beach. The people also used many remedies made from plants to cure their children, using dandelions, elderberries and so on; the only thing that made us bad as children was eating crab apples. They were bitter, but to us kids an apple was an apple and we could not resist them.

We were always out in the fresh air and our mothers hardly saw us except when we went home for meals. The fathers were the same. They were never around when our mothers wanted them, they were either beachcombing, duck hunting or sitting on the embankment talking, with a Woodbine in their mouths, watching where the coal was being shunted and noting what kind of coal it was (we only burned the best); later, when it was dark they would make a visit with a sack.

There was another street of houses on the dock, and this was called Wharf Row. To get there you had to cross Newbridge Road or come along the tramroad; the Row faced the town and its back was opposite the dry dock, with the railway sidings leading to the coal tipplers (hoists) between their back gardens and the dry dock. On the far side of the Row was the chemical plant and all day long there was a pong in the air that smelt like vinegar; opposite the plant was the Dock Hotel where you could have the best pint of Trumans in the town.

In front of the Row people had built a dance hall and they ran dances there every Saturday night. They also had concerts and pantomimes, and people came from Newbridge Road, Ruskin Avenue and Beach Hill to dance there. Ossie Morris and Llew Thomas brought the house down in their concerts. The Dock Police Station was there too, situated in the middle of the street, with Inspector Best as the officer in charge. His sergeants and constables were big men and patrolled the dock twenty-four hours a day.

Further up from the Dock Hotel was the Harbour House, and alongside this was the Seamen's Mission which was very active then. I am sorry to say that the only reason we went to the Sunday Services was because they gave tea and biscuits free. We did not tell our parents about this, but I think they knew, because we would have a quick wash (a 'lick and a promise') and our mothers would stand there in amazement because we washed twice that day!

I also remember the Phoenix Works which were built, but not completed until the Fuel Works opened up there, producing ovoids and pitch blocks. My father, my brothers and I all worked there, where the pitch dust hung over you all day long. Your face would burn all day long after having a wash, and in the summer especially all the heat would leave your face burnt red like a Red Indian. The best thing I ever did was to leave the Fuel Works. It was like working in Hell, and my first pay packet was 17/6, seventeen shillings and sixpence (87 ½ p), twelve and sixpence to my mother and five shillings for my pocket money.

Claude Hadley, Jack Purchase and their ladies arrived in the street unexpectedly one day after the war. They wanted to convert one of the air-raid shelters into some form of church for us children, and they worked hard on the shelters for some weeks till it was ready. On its first Sunday we were all cleaned up and dressed in our best clothes and we attended the first service. We could have been angels in Paradise, we enjoyed it so much; they put on concerts and held whist drives for the parents. Mr. Hadley and the others were wonderful people who really had come down to help us.

We had some lovely singers in the street. For instance, Marion Deare had a beautiful voice, and even the Dock Police, busy chasing Leonard Haines, stopped to listen to the choir singing on a Sunday.

We all, more or less, went to the Central School, except for the older boys who went to Eastern School. Later a Davies Brothers bus used to come to take us to school and bring us home at tea time, and this was the only transport we had. If we were going to the pictures (as we called the cinema then) our mothers would stand by until the bus arrived from school, then they would give us sandwiches wrapped in paper and a shilling for the outing – sixpence for the pictures and sixpence for chips. We would go back again with the bus to the Picturedrome (the 'Cach') or the Grand Cinema.

I always remember the Grand Cinema as a cold place. (We were told – and believed – that the rats wore coats and cwtched against our legs for warmth). Afterwards we would go to Ma Servini's café. The Picturedrome was a smaller cinema. We would go in the cheapest seats, which meant we were right in front of the screen, looking straight up at it, and after watching the film, we would go home with aching necks and looking like zombies! Before we went in, we would visit Jack Stevens's fruit shop for a penn'orth of cut-up apples. We also used to go to the magic lantern show at St. Theodore's, where we would watch silent films (mostly those of Charlie Chaplin).

It is nice to look back and enjoy the times when the ice-cream man came down with his horse and cart. It was a treat for us, as we ran to meet him up on the road – the poor horse didn't know what was happening, with a dozen children excitedly running alongside him. Another regular visitor was the milkman, with his milk churns; he would serve the milk into our jugs with a ladle. And Theodore the baker delivered bread door to door, locking his van up every time he left it; I don't think he trusted us much.

After the workmen went home we would go down to the pier, which had a narrow gauge line running down onto it. The workmen would have taken the trolley off this line and put it on one side, but we would pick it up and put it back, then push it down the line towards the hill on the pier. Next we would scramble on and ride the trolley down the hill. How there wasn't an accident, I'll never know, because the speed at which we travelled down that hill was breath-taking. We went on riding the trolley until somebody spotted the Dock Police peddling towards us at full speed in a cloud of dust. Then we would all jump over the pier (though only if the tide was out), and run like hell. The police could not catch us because they were out of breath from peddling uphill towards us from the lock gate.

Some of us boys would walk to Goytre from Dock Street to play football for the Goytre school boys' team. I remember their changing rooms were on the main road above the cemetery and the pitch was alongside the river and Glenhafod Colliery.

At other times we would watch the men playing pitch and toss, throwing pennies in the air and seeing the sun glittering on them as they fell to the ground, while we kept an eye out in case a policeman came along.

When somebody in the street got married, it meant great excitement for the children. The bride and groom would go to church to get married, and while they were gone the kids would be looking up the road, waiting for them. When they got back everybody would be outside and the groom would chuck pennies at the kids, followed by a terrible scramble. We kids would jump onto the window sills and peep into the house, which would be full of Woodbine smoke, with everybody laughing away, a glass of beer in their hand. They would be standing shoulder to shoulder, and the guests would be overflowing into the back garden, legs unsteady, ties off, beer in one hand, a fag in the other and a sandwich between their teeth. They would look up at a train of coal passing by, then somebody would shout, 'Just our bloody luck, with our best suits on!' The coal trains cruised by as they drank their pints, the locomotive driver waving and smiling.

Chapter Six

We all looked forward to the summer holidays from school. I can still remember the names (or nicknames) of some of the Central School teachers – Sid Vaughan the headmaster, Daddy Harris, Miss Davies and Pansy Rees. And every time I see Les Evans it reminds me of my time at the Central School.

It was the day when we were breaking up for the summer holidays. We had a baseball bat that someone had given us, and I was carrying this when Mr. Evans came past us. He asked what we were going to do with it, and we said that we were going to play baseball in the holidays. 'Somebody's going to have an accident before you come back,' he said, and sure enough we did.

We were playing rounders and Leonard Haines was batting. He hit the ball and threw the bat away as he was running; I ran in for my turn and the bat struck me and knocked me out. I came round while they were carrying me back to the street, and there was blood running down my face. I had a gash on my forehead, just above the eye, so they wiped me down and Johnny Coombes came to take me to hospital on the crossbar of his bike. I was still dazed, and he kept asking me if I was all right and telling me to hang on. After two miles like this, we arrived at the hospital, where they put six stitches in the wound. There were no cars then, because petrol was rationed, so I owed Johnny Coombes my thanks. Afterwards he took me home, with the biggest headache I ever had and a bandage wrapped round my head for the next week. I have never, never touched a baseball bat since!

Petrol was not the only thing that was rationed, and my mother had to exchange the coupons in our ration books sometimes because my brother Albert would not eat meat. All he would eat was cheese, and it was nothing for him to walk around with a lump of cheese in his hand as if it was an apple. Some people would sell their coupons to make ends meet, but the only thing that was not rationed was the rabbits.

We had no gas or electricity. Paraffin lamps and candles gave us light. We had no bath either, only the tin one hanging outside on the wall, but I remember those baths in front of the fire – jumping into the water after my brothers. The fireplace would be gleaming after our mother had spent the morning blackleading it. (On Friday nights we would hurry our bath so that we could listen to that day's episode of 'Dick Barton, Special Agent' on our dry battery wireless).

Then our mothers would start washing our dirty clothes, scrubbing by hand on a scrubbing board, then rinsing, then putting them through the mangle (with me turning the handle) and lastly putting our underwear and socks to air for the morning in the oven alongside the fireplace. I have also seen people putting little chicks in the warm oven to help them survive; the chicks came out later, cheeping around the place when we tried to catch them.

In the evenings, after their day's work was done, our mothers would group together in the street for a chat. They would lean on the window sills or sit on the pavements, with their babies wrapped in shawls, Welsh fashion (it was nothing to see them carry the babies all day like this). It was very rarely that you saw them go out with their husbands. After cleaning, washing by hand, cooking and feeding us, they did not have the strength to dress up and go for a drink. Their only enjoyment in those days was either the pictures (and they were a three-mile walk away) or the wireless. It was very different to today, when there are motor cars, bingo, television, electric light and plumbed-in baths.

There were twenty-five houses in the street and if any family was in trouble, they would all gather round and do what they could to help. If anyone's old man was sick, they would go to the coal wagons and fill his coalhouse before tea.

Most people in those days kept chickens, ducks or geese to help both their budget and the difficulties of rationing. We very rarely saw a coalman coming down to us, but if one did, we would try to sell coal to him. Otherwise the only people who did come down were the baker, the milkman and Thomas the Oil who sold boot polish, candles, paraffin and Brasso. I also remember a man called Mr. Hardtop, who ran a money club; you would pay in so much a week, then get your club out at a certain set time.

In the summers, when we spent all our time down at the beach, we would take dripping and jam sandwiches for food and a bottle of dewberry pop. This consisted of crushed dewberries in a bottle of water, with added sugar; it would be shaken well and then it was a beautiful drink. At the end of the day we would come home to a Dock Street special for our supper: fry-up left from dinner time and bread pudding.

During the war we all went to school with a gas mask in a cardboard box hung round our necks on a string. The box was very handy; we could hide a pack of cards in it, away from the teacher's eye – or even more Rennies – we used to eat Rennies instead of sweets because there were hardly any sweets about then. At least there was no way we could have had indigestion!

Now and again the pop men would come down to us and then the boys would hang on to the back of the lorry for a ride. On one particular time we all jumped off except for Bobby Morgan whose hand got caught on the back of the lorry. He was being dragged along, but his aunty was upstairs, leaning out to clean her window, and when she saw what was happening she screamed so loud that the lorry driver stopped at once. Bobby was a very lucky boy, and got away with bloody knees and a few scratches.

The town's refuse tip was where the steelworks sinter plant is now, and since it was only just up the road from the street, we would go up there scavenging around. We used to find an amazing mixture of things there – tailor's dummies, old furniture, pop bottles that we could take back for money and shoes. Sometimes we would find some good pairs of shoes and then we would sell them for a shilling a pair.

The tide used to come in right up to the tip and it was very dangerous then to look round it. (When I say the tide used to come in, I mean that the tide would come in through the Betsy Pool and up to the tip, filling all the pills right up to the edge of the road that led to the street). Sometimes the water would pour over the road. Once my brother Richard got stuck in the mud near the refuse tip and started to sink; he was up to his belly when some workmen came along, put tin sheets down and pulled him out. He was very lucky that those men came along.

The Whitsun Carnivals in the street were outstanding. The women would make chains out of daisies and buttercups to put round the girls' necks, and a Carnival Queen was chosen every year. She would parade up and down the street with her maids of honour, followed by the children who would have dressed up. Meanwhile tables would be brought out into the street and made ready for the feast; all the mothers baked for the occasion.

We looked forward to this every year as our only enjoyment except for our day trip to Barry Island in August. We picked dewberries for a month, then sold them and gave the money to Joyce Crealock to save for us.

In July and August we would pick dewberries all through the week and store them until the weekend, when our mothers would go up town and sell them to the owners of the market stalls. During the week, too, we boys and girls would go up town and sell the berries door to door for sixpence a pound or a pint glass. While we were doing this, we would be dodging the boardman (or school inspector). Our reward for all this work was the trip to Barry Island.

At Christmas time we boys would go around the dock after tea, singing Christmas carols, and looking back now I can remember how we would go coal-dust-blowing everywhere, singing to the workers at the coal Tipplers. We would approach their cabin while they were having their tea, then we would sing and the door would open. The room would be in darkness, with a big fire blazing at the far end, and I can still see today how we would go to the middle of the cabin and the workers would look up at us from their lunch boxes – and we could see only their white eyes staring at us from the darkness. I would feel as if we were in the middle of a forest at night, with the eyes of unseen beasts of prey staring at us, but we came away with a shilling in coppers and a dripping sandwich.

We would go out on to the foreign boats and sing too, and come away from them with cigarettes, salted butter and sugar, then we would go home freezing and give our gifts to our mothers – who would take them from us and give us a clip around the ear for going on the foreign boats. (But then my mother would turn and walk away with a grin!)

Sometimes we would go on the foreign ships in July and sing Christmas carols. The sailors didn't understand what we were singing about, so we got away with it and Leonard Haines, our leading tenor, would pocket the money. Then we would go up town and Leonard, the oldest boy, six feet tall, would share the takings out – one for you, two for me, one for you, two for me, and so on and on.

We played football too, nearly every day of the week. Some of the girls played with us, and one, I remember, Marion, left you feeling as if you had been hit by a rhinoceros when she tackled you. Another girl, Joanie, would kick your boots off with the laces still done up. Some of the boys were pretty good too, for instance Trevor Haines who later played in the Welsh League for Port Talbot and other clubs, and was a good, fast centre forward. And George Jenkins played for Cwmavon in the Welsh League; to pass him was like going through a brick wall.

Across the other side of the dock was the Dock Hotel, built about 1890. At first it was owned by the railway and on top of the hotel there was a glass dome, made of copper and brass. It was originally a look-out used for sighting sailing ships and as soon as the people at the hotel saw a ship coming in, they would light up all the hotel rooms and kindle the fires, ready for the passengers. Then, after the passengers had spent the night there, they could catch a train outside the hotel, at a station specially built for them. (The signal box for the station stood there for many years after the station itself had closed down. It was pulled down in the seventies).

After a while the hotel was sold to Trumans, and as far as I can discover, Mrs. Rees then took over as the landlady; later on her son Gwyn took over from her, and finally Mr. and Mrs. Watts took over from Gwyn Rees. The Dock Hotel kept one of the strongest pints in the town and many who had had too much either walked or fell into the dock, just missing the lock gates. Many thousands of seamen spent happy times there and the amount of contraband cigarettes, tobacco and whiskey that was passed under the table was nobody's business. The 'free and easy' in the back room would be packed with people, with Johnny Coombes as chairman.

I was there when the first woman captain stepped into the Dock Hotel. I think she was the very first woman captain to bring a ship into this country and the event was mentioned in the Daily Express. She was a Russian and her ship carried coil for the British Steel Company. I also remember the arrival of the last sailing ship. Her name was the 'Passat' and hundreds of people flocked down to see her berthed by the dry dock. She was carrying wheat from Australia, but entered the dock empty.

Chapter Seven

In the winter nights, when there was no street lighting and everything was dark, we would grab hold of a big oil drum and make holes in the sides, then jump on the nearest coal wagon, get some coal and light a big fire in the drum. To start the fire we would get an old can and take some oil out of the oil pots on the sides of the wheels of the coal trucks. Then we would stand around it all night, baking potatoes and talking about the films we had seen in the Grand, the Plaza or the Cach (Picturedrome). Or we might have a sing-song while the potatoes cooked, with Marion Deare leading us with her beautiful voice. The big boys smoked fags – Woodbine or Park Drive – and drank pop (Our Boys or Tizer) which was bought from Evan Jenkins's shop. If we ran out of potatoes, Leonard Haines, my brother Richard and Vivian Thomas would creep into some poor bugger's allotment for spuds. Sometimes a policeman would come along for a warm; he would bend down, warming his hands and looking at the fire, perhaps even saying 'What a lovely fire!' – and then when he got up, he would find he had been deserted.

We also played games on young railway checkers, who would be taking wagon numbers in the lonely sidings. They would work in between the wagons by the light of a torch and if they were young and new to the job, we would make noises like a ghost, calling out in a low voice, 'Are you there?' The torch would drop to the floor and the checker would be gone like a flash, while we sat on top of the wagons, laughing our heads off.

In certain places on the railway there were water tanks where the locomotives filled up with water, using a huge rubber hose, and there we would take off our clothes and turn the water on. It came out with such force that it nearly drowned us.

We were not always too clever in our games, and we had many a kick up the backside from the drivers and shunters. We would jump into an empty wagon and then perhaps an engine would come along and shunt the wagon into the sidings, flinging us about, especially when it was shunted against other wagons. Looking back, it's hard to see how we never had a serious accident.

One near-disaster in particular I remember. I was with my mother and Mrs. Phyllis Evans, two big women, waiting to cross the dock by launch. When the launch finally came alongside, its deck was slightly below the landing stage; the driver was watching this when my mother put me onto the boat, and he shouted 'Oh no!' when my mother and Mrs. Evans jumped on at the same time. The launch made a groaning sound and went right down in the water, as though it was going to sink. The boat bounced up and down like a beach ball, swerving back and forward at the same time, while the driver hung on to the controls, shouting to the two large women to sit down, one on each side of the launch.

It took a couple of minutes at least for the driver to get his nerve back, and he said he thought his time had come. I was in stitches, holding on to the cabin, while my mother and Phyllis Evans, each on their own side of the launch, looked at each other, then burst out laughing, while the driver guided the launch away, muttering to himself in the sort of language my mother forbade us to use.

There was another occasion when the dock workers were standing on the landing stage, waiting to get on the launch. At the front of the queue stood a small man with a hunch-back. The launch pulled up and a boy on the launch was going about his job, tying the boat up to steady it, when one of the men at the back of the queue shouted out, 'Come on, jump on.' The man with the hunch-back turned around, pointing at his hump, and said, 'What do you think this is? 'A bloody parachute?' A roar of laughter came from the waiting men as they realised the funny side of his comment.

It was a wonderful sight to watch the tugs pulling the iron-ore boats through the dock, passing Llewellyn Quay, turning the boat about by the Phoenix Wharf, and pulling it into position under the transporter, ready for discharging. Two ships would be berthed there at the same time while the transporter cranes discharged the cargoes with their huge grabs. There were times when the iron-ore ship was empty and we would creep on board, knowing that the ship had carried monkey nuts before. We would go down into the hold with our sacks and fill these with the left-over monkey nuts, finding these in the corners of the hold; then we would scarper out of the place before the Dock Police arrived. A lot of these iron-ore boats had names starting with 'K'; I think they were owned by the Steel Company of Wales, and I remember one called Ka Vic Joc.

Often we would sit on the sand tumps watching with much interest as the boats came in and out of the lock gates. We would watch the lock keepers running around with the lines, putting the ropes around the capstans to make the boat steady. If it was a small coal boat, they would put another boat alongside it, then the outer lock would slowly open towards the sea and Rolly Thomas, Ken Pugh, Bob Quick and Johnny Bartle, the keepers, would take the ropes off the capstans. Ken Pugh and Johnny Bartle were small men; they would run about in their blue uniforms and peaked caps, while Rolly Thomas and Bob Quick (a slight man, well over six feet tall) would open the gates.

Slowly the boats would creep out of the lock, with inches to spare. Then, after the boats had gone out, the tugs would do their duty by towing them out between the two piers, and one tug would stay behind each boat to steady it. It was a difficult job, especially when the weather was bad, and after all their work Rolly, Ken, Bob and Johnny could be seen slowly going over to the Dock Hotel for a well-earned pint before going home to wait for the next tide.

The men I admired were the crew of the pilot boat. They would go out in all kinds of weather and I often saw them going out in bad conditions, with a rough wind blowing. As they went outside the pier, they would go up and down with the waves, going down, then disappearing, then bobbing up on another wave until they reached the waiting ships outside. People talk about lifeboats going out in rough weather to rescue sailors, but these men were at it every day of the year, no matter what the conditions might be.

We would be down there on a rough day, with the wind blowing in our faces and the smell of salt water strong around us. The tugs would be blowing their hooters, while the waves from the swell of the ship's propellers battled up against the pier, and we would watch them being berthed alongside the coal tipplers. After the ships were berthed, the coal wagons would start to roll down from the sidings; one by one they would run on to the turntables, to be turned about, then moved on to the tippler to be hoisted up and tipped upside down until the wagon was empty. This continued until the ship was fully loaded. There would be clouds of dust everywhere and the faces of the men on the tipplers would be like black masks, with only the whites of their eyes showing.

It's odd looking back to the way the docks beach was organised then. Each street had its own patch. People from Wharf Row and Newbridge Road would come across the lock gates and swim by the stone pier, we people from Dock Street would swim in the middle of the beach, and those from Taibach and from West End would come through along the steelworks, cross the Betsy Pool if the tide was out, and swim near there.

We got on all right with the West End people, the Cardys, the Inskips and Davieses. Leyshon Thomas's shop was in West End, and we would go there to get something before we went to the pictures or to the magic lantern show at St. Theodore's to see Charlie Chaplin films.

We also played a lot of football with the boys from West End and Wharf Row, on a pitch we had made not far from the lock gates. There was a remarkable character from Wharf Row called Phil Beacham; he was a big man with a kick like a thunder-bolt, and if he hit you with one of his drives, you would end up in a sand tump with stars as big as dewberries in front of your eyes. Then he would pick you up like a sack of potatoes. He always drove about on a big motorbike, and he really loved that bike.

Then there were the Cardys, a large family with a wonder-ful mother. They lived at number one, West End, and were one of the biggest families in the town. Mrs. Cardy often visited my mother and we often went to visit her when our mother took us to Taibach; we would leave our bikes in her garden if we were going to the Cach (Picturedrome) or the Regent cinema.

There were other families too who lived in Dock Street, but moved away when I was very young: Groves, Freemans, Bamfords, McCanns, Perrings and Bartles.

Our favourite place was the beach, and in the summer we lived down there night and day. Camping out under the stars was something special. The big boys would camp in one spot and the smaller boys in another, then in the night the big boys would creep up and frighten the living daylights out of us, till in the end we ran home to Mama.

We did some wild things in those days. For instance, we used to go over to the docks and 'borrow' the rowing boats. The big boys would take one and row out into the middle of the dock, then the smallest boys would follow suit and row out into the darkness. We would be enjoying ourselves rowing about in the middle when all of a sudden we would hear 'Ho, Ho, heave ho!' and the big boys would row out of the darkness, ramming us head on. We shouted back at them, using the language we had already heard from them.

In the meantime the Dock Police had heard the noise, so they surrounded the dock, blowing their whistles. We rowed slowly towards Margam Wharf, making our way there under the shadow of the darkness, like the 'Cockle Shell Heroes' in the film, and waited under the jetty until the police had given up. Then we would go home.

Another of our 'adventures' happened when we went to the pictures in town. We would wait for a loco which was taking empty wagons back to the collieries, then we would jump onto the guards' van and hang on until we came to the Eastern School at Taibach where we would jump off. Sometimes the guard would see us, and shout at us to get off and the only way to keep him in the guards' van was to throw coal at him. We would do the same on the journey home, though it was a bit awkward to try to hold on with one hand and eat chips with the other.

Our mothers made an art out of trying to get us in for bed at night. Sometimes they would stand on the sand tumps calling our names: 'Tom, come on! Trevor, come on! Joanie, where are you? Leonard, where the bloody hell are you? If you don't come, I'll send your father after you!' They sounded like Swiss yodellers standing on top of a mountain.

We were very lucky to live in a street surround by wild life. First there were the otters, which we often saw by night, but rarely by day. They could be seen sliding down the banks into the pills, moving noiselessly in the water, smooth, beautiful animals that never harmed anybody. Then there were the hares and rabbits that burrowed in the large warren in front of the street and in the dunes and railway sidings. It was a way of life in the street to hunt the rabbits for Sunday dinner – at least until myxomatosis came along in later years.

Then there were all the birds. There was the common curlew, about two feet long, with a four to six inch bill, which would run along the sands all day. And hundreds of geese landed at the Betsy Pool; we would sit on the sand tumps watching them. In the winter they could be seen in their hundreds, coming from the Scandinavian countries, Norway, Sweden, Finland, and sometimes, so they said, from as far away as Russia. They were noisy, and when they landed you could hear them sounding as if they were talking to you. The most familiar sight of all was the wild ducks, mallards especially; large numbers would fly over in a V formation, and at night you would hear the hunters' guns going off at the Betsy Pool, bang, bang!

Among the thistles on the sides of the railway embankments and the sand tumps were the beautiful goldfinches, and there were green finches and chaffinches too. The finches are birds with beaks specially adapted for crushing seed and they were our favourite birds. Some people would catch them with a net and cage them, and some would even go as far as selling them. We also watched the linnets, birds that whistle and sing all day; we knew that whenever they were around, the finches were not far away. Then there were the birds of the thrush family which could often be seen only inches from the street in cold weather, waiting for us to throw crusts for them; they were the birds that came closest to us in the winter.

We used to sit on a sand tump at the Betsy Pool and watch the Steel Company locos pulling the ladles up to Morfa Bank, then tipping balls of red hot slag down the bank, one at a time, into the tide. We would watch the ball of slag rolling down the slope, then, as it hit the water, there would be a loud explosion like a bomb going off, followed by a cloud of steam everywhere. This explosive banging continued all through both day and night, but it was something we got used to in Dock Street.

Even the wild life got used to the explosions. In front of our street, towards Morfa Bank, was the warren where we could pick mushrooms, water cress and water lilies, or stand by the pills and watch the otters swimming about and the badgers. Peewits would be dancing round, trying to put us off while we looked for their eggs, then there were the beautiful gold-finches pecking away at the thistles and seagulls making a fuss above us.

It wasn't always like this, though. In the winter there was no shelter to protect the street; the wind and rain would come in from the sea, right across us, and we would hear the famous cries of 'Shut the front door' or 'If you go out the back, close the door after you.' These words were what we heard in the wind, messages from our parents. Sometimes, though, we would wake up with joy, finding snow had fallen, and go out with happy faces, to play all day.

There was not much to do in the winter after coming home from school, because it was dark by the time we had had our tea. Some of the games we played were 'Hullah Baloo' or 'Jack, Jack, show the light'; or we might go out to stock up on coal for the week. That was a bit dodgy in the dark, when every time we saw a telegraph pole somebody would shout 'copper!' and we would drop the coal and run like hell. That is what we got up to as children, fifty years ago.

Chapter Eight

Gone now are the days when paddle steamers regularly picked up hundreds of passengers outside the lock gates. People came from all over the Valleys to sail on these trips around the Bristol Channel and it was a fantastic sight to see the ship's paddles ploughing through the water as it headed between the stone pier and the wooden pier and towards the lock gates.

Gone too is the sound of the hooters every morning; they would sound the times of every shift, starting at 6 a.m., then at 7 and 8 a.m. And another sound that is no more is the noise of railway wagons banging against the buffers as they were shunted into the sidings, with the engines puffing away, pushing the wagons full of coal up the inclines (or high banks). The convoy would get half way up, then skid and run back down, then start again. All this went on at the back of our street while we were trying to sleep.

On February 1st, 1945, a Thursday, a sad accident created much pain in the town. This happened at a siding crossing, as a bus was carrying workmen home from work. I believe the bus tried to beat a locomotive across the siding and a collision occurred when the loco caught the tail end of the bus. Two men were killed outright, four died in hospital and five others were injured badly enough to be rushed to hospital. Of those killed, three came from Cwmavon, one from Margam and two from town.

The accident happened after we had passed the place in the school bus which was taking us home from school. We heard about it later, and we boys went back to look. I remember watching the crane picking up the bus, and the police keeping us back while we shivered in the cold wind blowing along the dock.

On a happier note, I remember when we went across the Betsy Pool to Morfa to try to see them making a film there. It was a war film about British soldiers being lost in the desert, and it was called 'Nine Men'. We did not stay long because the tide was coming in and we had to get back across the Betsy

Pool. I believe the actors stayed at the Grand Hotel. One of the actors became famous; his name was Gordon Jackson, and I believe this was one of his first films. Some people from town took part in the film as extras.

I remember the winter of 1947, when everything was at a standstill. The dock was frozen over, and down on the beach the waves froze and were left there after the tide had gone out. All the railway wagons were frozen to the rails, nobody could cross the lock gate, and since the launch was also trapped in the ice in the dock, we had to walk three miles, up to our waists in snow, to get to town for milk, bread and groceries.

Many thousands of birds died that winter and I remember thrushes walking up, into our hands, to be fed. We hardly saw a rabbit, and the few we did see had thick fur coats. Coal was scarce too, unless you had a pick. There was no school and for weeks we skated on the ponds. The sand tumps were like white mountains and we made sledges so that we could slide down them. We were thrilled with this freedom – until one day, to our horror, the school bus arrived and our un-official holiday was over.

In April that year, on one terrible stormy night, I remember rockets being fired down by Morfa Beach; to our horror the whole crew of the Samtampa and of the Mumbles lifeboat went down on the rocks at Sker. The following morning we went down to see the wreck which was cut clean in half.

My wife lived in Tŷ Canol, Cwmavon, at the time of that dreadful night. Her mother, Mrs. Gwendoline Gibbs, got up in the morning, went out into the garden and called out to her daughter Marjorie to come and look. My wife went out and her mother pointed at the bushes, which were covered with oil. They did not know about the disaster at Sker Rock the night before, but my future mother-in-law said, 'Some poor bugger at sea has had it.' When they went back into the house, they heard on the radio that the Samtampa had gone down, and also the lifeboat, with the loss of all hands.

On Sunday, March 12th, 1950, we were playing football when suddenly the largest plane we had ever seen passed over us, flying very low and swaying from side to side. We guessed that they were supporters coming back from Ireland after watching Wales play over there, and somebody said, 'Look, they're drunk and dancing up there!' We went home for tea and learned from the radio that the same plane had crashed at Llandow aerodome. We could hardly believe it, but some eighty-seven people perished in that disaster.

I remember one day in nineteen fifty three when I was home on leave from the Army and we all went from the street to see our first Cup Final live on television at the Dock Hotel. Gwyn Rees, the landlord, had one of the first television sets to be installed in Port Talbot and he put it in the back room where he held his 'Free For All-Night' concerts. That Saturday it was jam packed with dockers, steelworkers, railway workers and us from Dock Street – and I don't think anybody worked on the dock that afternoon.

We were packed in like sardines, with Will the Fish jumping up and down, while Sid Walton had lost his walking stick and Eddy Richards and Albert Parsons were sitting in front, refereeing the game, with two pints each so that they wouldn't have to get up and risk losing their seats. Gwyn Rees was smiling all afternoon as they drank and watched his black and white miracle. After a while windows were opened to let out the Park Drive and Woodbine smoke; it was so thick that the colour of the walls had changed from white to brown by the end of the night.

When half time arrived, everybody scrambled for the toilet which was on the far side of the bar, at the corner of the front bar. (It was one of those toilets you needed an overcoat to go into, it was as cold as a freezer in a butcher's shop). Then it was back to the game, and Phil Beacham banged the table, shouting out 'Bloody foul!' Someone else called out 'Shut up, you blind bat!' Everybody laughed out loud and Will Smith hung on to his pint to stop it spilling over.

The game came to an end, and it was 'Stop-tap.' Everybody went home happy and merry, walking in groups, some on their bikes, wobbling all over the road. That was the first time we saw live television, with a beautiful pint of Trumans in our hands and Gwyn Rees the landlord smiling behind us as we went out.

Chapter Nine

Dock Street has gone now. It was pulled down in 1955, while I was in the Army. I was told that many of the people broke their hearts and some refused to move and a railway worker who had seen it all said that watching them move out with their furniture on horse and carts or lorries was a very moving sight. 'The poor buggers will miss the coal,' he commented.

It was in 1970 that the Port Talbot Dock ceased to function. The railway stopped, the coal tipplers were dismantled and there was an end to the days when you could walk past the dry dock and see hundreds of men working on a ship – it was like watching the little men of Lilliput climbing all over Gulliver. The workmen would be tapping, banging and rivetting, lights were flashing as the welders worked; then, when the hooter went for dinner, everything stopped dead. The men would scramble out and run to Powells for Woodbines and a cup of tea – though some would run to the Dock Hotel for a quick one. The Dock Hotel has also gone, though it was a fine building that should never have been knocked down; it should have turned into something like a Dock Museum.

Other places too have disappeared: Wharf Row, with its dance hall (I recall many memorable times at the dances), and the Dock Police Station. Only Powell's building where the dock workers had their cups of tea, buns and cigarettes and the engineering shop called Galliver's, which is run by Mr. Powell's son, still survive; the buildings are over a hundred years old.

When the time came for the people of Dock Street to move, I think everybody in the street refused to leave at first. The council sent messengers down, time after time, to persuade the people to go and they made many promises: for instance, that we would all be rehoused together, in the same street and the rent would be the same. In their hearts the people knew that they would have to go in the end; they could not stop progress and Dock Street would have to be knocked down to make way for development at the steelworks.

However, the council's promises were not fulfilled. The people were distributed all over the new Sandfields estate, sometimes as much as a quarter of a mile from their old neighbours, and the rent was doubled.

Certainly it was a huge novelty for them, having electricity and gas for the first time, a bath that never moved, a toilet that was indoors – and upstairs too! – hot running water, and a modern fireplace when our mothers were used to blackleading their old coal fireplaces. But freedom had gone out of our lives for good – no more roaming the warrens for rabbits or going to pick dewberries.

It was the older people I felt sorry for – they were stuck in a house with a view of houses facing them front and back, after living in what had been a paradise for them (and a healthy one at that). Even the Dock Police must have missed us: no more chasing 'coalnappers', no more worrying where they put their bikes; Haines, Parsons, Crealock, Evans; all the families out of their way at last. Of those still left, many are now in their seventies, eighties or even nineties: Joyce Crealock, Evan Jenkins, Annie Jenkins and Dai McCarthy (who married Beryl Deare).

Port Talbot Docks

Over a hundred years of toil and sweat,
Until in the Seventies came the threat.
The Port Talbot Dock is now empty:
It ceased to function in Nineteen Seventy.

Gone are the sailing ships of old,
Gone are the steam ships so bold.
From the south the winds blow angry towards the port,
Up against the locks that will never see another boat.

Away went the last ship so brave,
Leaving the lock gates with a wave;
Ken Pugh and Bob Quick were lock keepers, mates –
For the last time they closed the gates.

The four keepers shook hands for the last time
And went to the Dock Hotel to spend their last dime.
From the Rio Tinto to Llewellyn's Quay
A launch would take you across for a fee.

Down came Wharf Row so proud,
Watched by Inspector Best in the crowd.
He watched his police station disappear in a cloud,
Thinking of all the summonses he made so loud.

They dismantled the coal tipplers and took them away,
Leaving the coal trimmers drawing their last pay.
The Dock Hotel where many pay packets opened with joy,
Where I took my first pint as a man, not a boy.

Oh, what a thrill, being there on Saturday night,
Playing dominoes, with the fire glowing so bright.
At number one tip stood the Tiddlywink
Where seamen once came over for a drink.

The old lock can still be seen today
By the Harbour House not far away.
The dock is closed and not a ship in sight.
The only thing that moves is a seagull in flight.

Just One of those Nights

With a balaclava over our heads
And wishing we were in our beds,
We walked along the railway tracks,
Looking for coal to fill our sacks.
It was cold and dark this night;
Our dog barked and gave us a fright.
We continued on, white as a ghost,
Until we walked into a telegraph post.
We limped on towards the coal.
Under my shoe was a hole.
We waited a minute or two
While I put a label in my shoe.
Making sure it was all clear,
We climbed the wagons near,
Filled our sack without a sound;
We lowered them to the ground.
'Somebody's coming,' came a yell.
We left everything and ran like hell.
Someone chased us along the tracks
Until he fell over our sacks.
Down the bank we jumped in haste,
Ending up in a pond, up to our waist.
We looked up to see our dog
Staring down at us in the bog;
Whispering for him to come down,
He stood there like a bloody clown.
With him barking there,
We bolted like a hare.
Home we went, so brave and bold,
No coal, and freezing cold!

Dock Street

Dock Street, a place of welcome and open arms,
A happy place with green fields and one farm,
A place where rabbits ran free,
A place where we had not one tree.

Tom Keogh had plenty of land at hand;
This Irishman always shouted 'Get off me land!'
Coal was always plenty and free;
We filled our coalhouse before tea.

Mrs. Tooze at number two sold pop and sweets,
Dai Williams at number one protected our street.
We had paraffin lamps and candles for light.
We listened to 'Dick Barton' every Friday night.

The Dock Hotel's got the best pint in town;
Many had one too much and fell down;
Truman's was the pint that got to your head –
The morning after, you wish you were dead!

We crossed the dock by launch for one penny fee;
If Harry Purchase drove the launch, we got across free.
Albert Parsons got involved in a fight –
He had his revenge by the launch one night.

Anybody who got in trouble or in a fix,
Billy Thomas would help if you knocked number six.
A barrack room lawyer he would often be;
If you had a summons, he was the one to see.

Tom Keogh's hay was set alight one day;
I wonder who did it in that month of May?
Evan Jenkins turned his shed into a shop.
We went to the beach for firewood to chop.

They shunted wagons all day long.
We took coal, which we knew was wrong;
Watching a loco pulling coal wagons through the rain,
Like Red Indians we attacked that train.

The driver tried to go as fast as he can –
The faster he went, the faster we ran.
Jumping on to a moving wagon was a work of art.
Like the Dock Hotel player they threw a good dart.
Ice-cream came down to us by horses and carts,
Theodore the baker delivered bread and tarts.

Watching our mother washing all day long,
Using a scrubbing board with a song;
Blackleading the fireplace was their pride,
While the eggs and bacon fried.

Hanging outside was the bath on the wall.
Saturday night was a bath for all –
Boiling water over a coal fire took time,
Us boys and girls bathing was a crime.

Violet had a turn and ran naked towards the beach!
The full moon shone that night; her backside shone like a
    peach.

The Dock Street Story

We picked dewberries all the week
Until our backs began to creak;
The seagulls knew, fluttering over our street,
That Dewberry Tart was for sweet.

Bread Pudding filled us up so we could not run –
Drop it and your big toe came up like a bun;
Some called it the 'Dock Street Wedding Cake'.
Believe that – you deserve to fall in Harvey's Lake.

Sunday was a day of rest,
Supper was fry-up at its best.
Whitsun treat came to us with joy,
Especially Johnny Brennan dressed up as a boy.

We often argued over whose turn it was to go for coal,
Especially when we knew Sergeant Webber was on patrol.
Men played Pitch and Toss against the walls,
Watched by the women with babies in their shawls.

When the meat coupons ran out in our book
We went down the warren for a rabbit to cook.
We found one, me and my mates;
Dinner time it landed on our plates.

We had an air-raid shelter for cover,
In case the Germans came over;
Over they flew with their load,
Dropped it right on our bloody road.

In the house we had no loo,
A bucket on the landing had to do.
After a pint we filled it every time –
Missing the bucket was a serious crime.

We watched the ships entering the dock;
Along came Mag and fell in the lock.
They pulled her out with a curse –
And in her hand she still held her purse.

Before we could walk, we learned to bend
Under railway wagons to the end.
Some clever engine drivers came past very fast,
Until we greased the line. And now it's in the past.

Agnes

She rose with the early sun
To take the cows for their run.
A cowgirl at heart,
Who could drive a horse and cart.
She drove the cows through the street,
Wearing wellies on her feet.
She was happy as a skylark
As they followed her home in the dark.
With her sisters they were eleven
Who lived at number seven,
In a street out in the wild
Where she grew up as a child.

Morfa Beach

Morfa Beach is no more a golden sandy beach.
 It's now ruined by an industrial leech;
Once happy families came down for the day –
 Now even the seagulls stay away.

Instead of sand tumps,
 Now they've got coal dumps.
It was a place to go and relax,
Now it's gone like the poll tax.

Once the beach was nice and clean;
 Now the black slag is there to be seen.
Once lapwings, kingfishers and rabbits roamed this land,
 Now it's black sludge that's got out of hand.

The Blackwood was a place of beauty and rare trees –
 Go down there now, it's like a dead carcass eaten by fleas.
The Margam moor streams once flowed free and clear –
 Now it's neglected, and for the fish to fear.

The harbour stretches out into the bay,
 The beach itself is nothing but clay;
The friends of the earth have hauled up a black flag
 Because Morfa Beach is nothing but a mass of slag.

Dock Stars about 1908 – Jim Herbert (sitting front, middle)

DOCK STREET CORONATION STREET PARTY, 1936
L-R: Mr. Crealock and his daughter Joyce; Johnny Coombes; John McCarthy; Florrie Jenkins *(behind);* Two ladies; Will Richard; Frank Freeman; Will McCarthy; Eddie Richard *(sitting)*

George Jenkins, Albert Haines and John Evans, outside the Street

Myself as a Blacksmith striker, with Gwilym Williams, Blacksmith, 1951

My brother Raymond, at the bottom of Dock Street

Will Evans as Lady Godiva
Dock Street Carnival

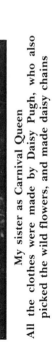

My sister as Carnival Queen
All the clothes were made by Daisy Pugh, who also
picked the wild flowers, and made daisy chains

My Sister being crowned as Carnival Queen
by Claude Hadley

Lyn Locke in the Street

My Mother *(on the left)* and Verna Brennan

Old Mr. Willment with his granddaughter in their back garden.
(Note the engine pulling a coal wagon, and their bath outside)

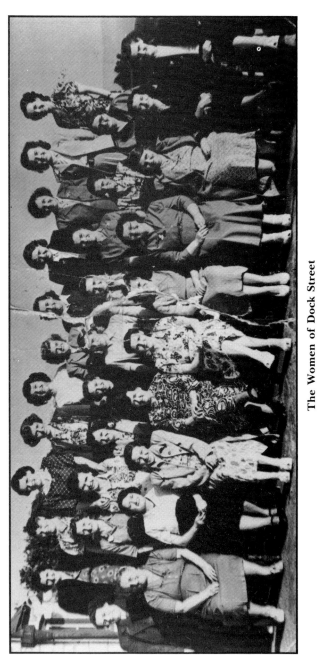

The Women of Dock Street

The Author at 17, before joining
the Army

Dock Steet ends after 57 years

An Air-Raid shelter like the one we used in 1940-42